A New True Book

SHIPS AND SEAPORTS

By Katharine Carter

*This "true book" was prepared
under the direction of
Illa Podendorf,
formerly with the Laboratory School,
University of Chicago*

CHILDRENS PRESS, CHICAGO

Loading a freighter

PHOTO CREDITS

Harbor House Productions—2, 9 (2 photos), 10
(2 photos: ship view photos), 13, 14, 15 (2 photos),
16, 17 (2 photos), 18 (2 photos: ship view photos),
25 (sea view photo), 26 (sea view photo), 29 (2
photos), 42 (sea view photo)

Port of Chicago—44

The Metropolitan Museum of Art Excavations,
1919-20; Rogers Fund, supplemented by
contributions of Edward S. Harkness—4

Lynn M. Stone—32 (bottom left)

James P. Rowan—6 (top), 32 (top)

Chicago Fire Department—34

Courtesy of National Archives—6 (bottom)

The Port Authority of New York and
New Jersey—36, 38, 40

Cunard Line—20 (bottom), 21, 23 (2)

Art Thoma—32 (bottom right)

Jerry Hennen—20 (top)

Jerome Wyckoff—30

H. G. Weis—Cover

Library of Congress Cataloging in Publication Data

Carter, Katharine Jones, 1905-
  Ships and seaports.

  (A New true book)
  Rev. ed. of: The true book of ships and
seaports. © 1963.
  Includes index.
  Summary: Briefly describes ships from the vessels
used by settlers to the efficient cargo vessels
and floating hotels in use today, and discusses
seaports and harbors.
  1. Ships—Juvenile literature. 2. Harbors—
Juvenile literature. [1. Ships. 2. Harbors]
I. Title.
VM150.C37 1982   387.2   82-4463
ISBN 0-516-01656-3   AACR2

TABLE OF CONTENTS

This wooden model of an Egyptian ship was built about 4,000
years ago. It was found in a tomb in Egypt.

EARLY SHIPS

The first sailing ships were built almost five thousand years ago. The Egyptians were the first to put sails on their ships. Ships have changed since then. But ships with sails have been built ever since.

Above: Three-masted sailing ships used about 300 years ago
Below: Early steamship

6

Ships have always been important.

People built ships to go from place to place. They used ships to cross oceans and to carry goods all over the world.

The first steamship went to sea almost two hundred years ago. But fast sailing ships continued to carry goods for another seventy-five years.

CARGO SHIPS TODAY

Ships that carry things from one place to another are called merchant ships.

The things that merchant ships carry are called cargo.

Ships that carry dry cargo are called freighters.

Some freighters are built to carry one kind of cargo.

Two different kinds of cargo ships

Tankers

Ships that carry liquid cargo are called tankers.

Tankers have tanks. These tanks hold millions of gallons of liquid cargo.

A tanker may carry oil, gasoline, molasses, or fruit juice.

Tanks are heated to keep a cargo of crude oil from becoming thick. They may be cooled if they are carrying orange juice.

A tanker has a pump room.

The cargo is pumped into the ship from tanks on shore. It is unloaded in the same way.

Freighters are loaded in many different ways.

Tanker going through a lock. Locks must be built when the water level of one body of water is higher, or lower, than the water level of the other body of water. When the lock gates are closed the water level can be raised or lowered. This allows ships to pass from one body of water to the other safely.

Cranes on a cargo ship

General cargo ships
have cranes aboard them.
The cranes lift the cargo
on and off.

These ships carry boxes
and bales, automobiles,
animals, machinery—all
kinds of things.

Above: Cargo ship
unloading
Left: Crane on
dock loads
cars onto a
cargo ship

Limestone being loaded

Loading corn

A large freighter can
carry 400,000 bushels of
grain. The grain is loaded
through pipes from bins on
the dock.

Coal and iron ore are
loaded in this same way.

Long ships carry iron
ore.

A seatrain is a freighter that has railroad tracks on its decks. Railroad cars are run onto the ship. Big elevators move the cars from one deck to another.

USS *United States*

Queen Elizabeth II

LINERS

Big oceangoing ships
that carry people are
called liners.

Liners are like hotels on
water. Some are as long
as two city blocks. They
have dining rooms,
libraries, and shops.

They have swimming pools, gyms, and movie theaters.

A large liner can carry two thousand passengers.

Another thousand people, the crew, work on the ship.

TUGBOATS

Tugboats are strong little boats. Day and night they push and pull ships around the harbors.

Huge ropes, or even tires, on the sides of the tugs act as bumpers.

Sometimes two or three tugs work together. They nose in against a big ship and push it in to the dock.

A tug can be a big ship's best friend. If a big ship is in trouble, a tug will go out and help it into the port.

Tugs also pull or push flatboats. These flatboats have no engines or sails. They are called barges.

Some barges carry cargo. They can carry coal, grain, cement, or sand. Some of them carry garbage.

Fishing boats at a wharf

FISHING BOATS

There are many kinds of fishing boats. One kind is a trawler. Trawlers carry large cone-shaped nets. The nets are dragged along the bottom of the ocean. Tons of fish are caught at one time.

Machinery on the deck pulls a net up into the ship.

Fishing boats

Lobster boats

Shrimp boats

Some tuna boats use another kind of net. A man in a small rowboat holds one end of the net. As the big boat makes a circle, the net rolls off a turntable on the stern. A rope in the bottom of the net can be drawn up. This makes the net into a bag where the fish are caught.

This bag net is called a purse.

FIREBOATS

All big seaports have fireboats. They are fire engines on water.

Fireboats can pump water from the sea and shoot it a long way.

Ships load and unload cargo at seaports

SEAPORTS

Seaports are homes for ships. Ships come into them to load and unload.

Seaports are safe places in a storm.

Port of New York

Seaports have long wooden and steel platforms called piers or docks. These reach out over the water. Many of them have railroad tracks on them.

From the air you can see the city of New York and its waterfront.

New York City has one of the largest seaports in the world. There are other large seaports in countries all over the world.

The largest seaports can hold hundreds of ships. They have hundreds of miles of waterfront and hundreds of miles of piers.

Ships come to these large seaports from all over the world.

Some seaports have piers built for unloading certain things.

Railroad cars can be loaded at the piers. Huge cranes move back and forth. They dip into the ship and lift out the cargo.

In some ports, small workboats line the piers. The boats are loaded with fish or crabs. Some of them bring in oysters and clams from the bottom of the rivers and bays.

Now we have trains and planes and trucks to carry freight. But many things still travel by cargo ships.

Ships and seaports are still very important to us.

WORDS YOU SHOULD KNOW

bale(BAIL) —a large, tightly wrapped bundle.

barge(BARJ) —a boat with a flat bottom used to carry cargo.

bin —an enclosed space for storing food, coal, or other items.

bumper(BUM • per) —something used to protect against being hit.

cargo(CAR • go) —freight; goods carried by a ship, truck, or other vehicle.

crane(CRAIN) —a large machine used to lift heavy objects.

crew(CROO) —the workers who run a ship or aircraft.

crude oil(CROOD) —oil that has not been refined, raw.

deck(DEK) —the floor of a ship.

freighter(FRAY • ter) —a ship that carries cargo.

harbor(HAR • ber) —a sheltered place where ships dock.

iron ore(EYE • ern OR) —rock that has iron in it.

liner(LYE • ner) —a ship that carries passengers.

merchant ship(MER • chent SHIP) —a ship that carries cargo.

pier(PEER) —a platform built over water from a shore where ships can tie up to.

purse net —a kind of net in which fish are caught.

stern(STIRN) —the rear part of a ship; away from the bow.

tanker(TANK • er) —a ship that carries liquid cargo.

trawler(TRAW • ler) —a type of fishing boat.

tugboat(TUG • boat) —a powerful small boat that tows or pushes large ships.

turntable(TERN • tay • bil) —a round platform that rotates.

INDEX

About the Author

Katharine Carter's long association with elementary students ended with her retirement from the Baltimore school system. Her move to a home on the shore of the Piankatank River fulfilled a lifetime dream. Mrs. Carter and her husband enjoy fishing, crabbing, gardening and reading.